ELEGIAC

ELEGIAC

Charles Seluzicki

The Cox Family Poetry Chapbook Series

Carnegie Mellon University Press
Pittsburgh 2021

Acknowledgments

The elegy for Jack Walsdorf first appeared as a memorial broadside printed by Andre Chaves at The Clinker Press in 2018.

The two first lines of "Hymn to Thanatos" are a variant of a moment in Paul Merchant's translation of Catullus, poem 3, his lament for Lesbia's sparrow. And thank you, Paul, for your valued counsel.

Cover photograph of a detail from Père Lachaise Cemetery, Paris, by Christina Seluzicki.

The author extends his gratitude to Ross Hamilton for technical assistance with the cover photo.

Elegiac by Charles Seluzicki is the first volume in The Cox Family Poetry Chapbook Series of Carnegie Mellon University Press. The Press administrators and staff express our profound appreciation to Courtney, Lisa, and Jordan Cox for their generous support.

Book design by Connie Amoroso

Printed in the United States of America

10   9   8   7   6   5   4   3   2   1

Library of Congress Cataloging-in-Publication Data

Names: Seluzicki, Charles, 1946- author.
Title: *Elegiac* / Charles Seluzicki.
Description: Pittsburgh : Carnegie Mellon University Press, 2021. | Series: The Cox family poetry chapbook series; volume 1 | Summary: "In his uncompromisingly intelligent and humane book of poems, Elegiac, Charles Seluzicki has delivered a late-breaking heartfelt and startlingly beautiful book of poems that seeks to remember and celebrate the lives of dear ones lost to him —Michael Dickman" —Provided by publisher.
Identifiers: LCCN 2020041025 | ISBN 9780887486708 (trade paperback)
Subjects: LCGFT: Poetry.
Classification: LCC PS3619.E46845 E44 2021 | DDC 811/.6--dc23
LC record available at https://lccn.loc.gov/2020041025

Contents

The Angel of Death

Can you truthfully say
With your last dying breath
That you'll be ready to meet
The Angel of Death?
  —Hank Williams

Wait! The Angel of Death
Has been busy of late,
Visiting upon the weary
One by one, creating
Special forms of loneliness.
His shadow visits multitudes.
I do not attribute this
To meanness. It is his job.
Our problem is love
And pity, robbed as we are
Of shared memory and time
And, yes, suddenly, solace.
Echoes of how many voices,
Now softer, touch the heart?
Wind-fallen fruit sweetening
The air. But you are not there.

7

Hymn to Thanatos

And now they are on that unlit road
They say no traveller retraces
And they leave with stories now untold
The privacies, captive, the pending cases.

Death, I've asked brother Sleep's guidance,
Or tried. Your smirk is troubling though.
I wonder at your talent for games of chance,
Hear the clatter of roulette wheel slow.

I begin to list the dead but hesitate.
Who can keep up? The young are understanding.
It is that time of life. Steely fate's
Edge glistens. Master, I am prostrate.

Not to submit, Master, is folly.
But you know the drill. Parry, retreat.
We'll do this for a while. And after
I'll share a story. The circle, complete.

Elegiac

With the farming of a verse
Make a vineyard of the curse
—W. H. Auden, In Memory of W. B. Yeats

How is it that a heavy heart
Appears the first requirement of Art?

And only after, Joy might forestall
Bits of sorrow in the wake of the Fall.

Death, a curse? The shadows of words
Are ever present. They scold.

And you all, yes, each and all,
Heard in every passing season a call.

Townsman of a stiller town

—A. E. Housman

I. Mark Strand

Marco! How you despised the obvious.
Rather, San Gimignano. This wine. A kiss.

Youth, aquiline and eternal. The heart's heat,
The womanly earth, the sweetness of peat.

Love's suddeness untempered by age,
Never betrayed your classical bent, the parade

Of forms that colored your ear or trained
Your line. The arts of painting, your refrain.

That famous difficulty now seems a virtue.
Come close now. I want to watch you.

Memory now my faithful correspondent, better
Than you in life, for sure, ever the debtor.

I never took it personally. A veil of irony
Clothed even your perfect happiness, colonized

The past, home and work. You told,
"Of occasions flounced with rose and gold."

II. Katherine Dunn

Sometimes I wondered how you did it.
The loneliness, the bills, the moonlit

Burden of words carried through your day,
The arts of motherhood and fiction played

Out offstage. You wiped your lenses
The way marksmen fix their sights

And considered the weight of words,
Bridling their animal fury, their deferred

Possibilities. Such eloquence is rare,
Katherine. Instead your flair

For uncertainty, cigarettes
And coffee served you best

Just as the mysteries of violence
Evidenced the ever-mounting sense

You continued to make of the world:
It was your pleasure. You heard

An echo of ideas ancient and near
Freshly, and with a reverence here,

In our time and place. I see you once
again, the prescient pause, the silence.

How reclaim the clarity, the freshets of breath
Drawn now through windowless veils of death?

III. Martin Stone

Those nights on Ménilmontant!
Such excess, ten scant

Years on the razor's edge. Oh!
You flew from the second floor,

Le deuxième étage your stage.
If only we had the footage.

It was 3 a.m. You knew the open bars.
Silhouettes on streets too small for cars,

Our private danger and personal noir.
The next day I stopped at every pissoir.

Finally, Martin, it caught up with you—
You called, "I feel so sick, so blue . . ."

And that was that. Ten short years to match
Those lost. The music, the books, a patch-

Work of everything that was ever fine.
How is it about endings and time?

Everything happens so fast.
Even now it is difficult to grasp

The eclipse in our extended conversation
The final jaunt and "It's cancer."

Distance impedes understanding.
The last time we spoke I knew a thing

Or two that I had feared admitting:
Your course was run, submitting

Seemed better than fighting. You were too
Weak. Word of your death shot me straight through.

IV. Jack Walsdorf

Books were your pleasure, completely.
I never saw anything like it. Fleeting

Spectacles of innovation never deterred
Your devotion to Morris. It conferred

The adventure of an aesthetic with grace,
A way of life. Variety kept pace

With tradition, beauty born of the crafts
Of the hand and eye, the past renewed

On the page. Aldus, Bodoni, Caslon . . .
An alphabet of classic typography rekindled

In the here and now. Your delight seemed
Inexhaustible. Your smile impish and serene.

How you reveled in the minutiae of the printer's
Art, the home team, all things Wisconsin,

& Oxford too. As a graver poised on endgrain,
Your friendships were crafted, sustained,

Etched with that promise of permanence
Honoring shared bonds, shared sense.

Still, each of us bears a necessary sadness.
And yours was great and then greater still.

I never quite knew but came to know well.
No one should have to lose a child. Your will

Seemed broken the last time I saw you.
But I never thought you might not pull through.

V. Louis McElroy

Your sense of things, Lou, was already refined.
I felt clumsy in such company. Time

Has only sharpened my hold on your openness
To the world of feeling. Doubt, duress,

You held them at bay—no other apart,
Trusting the purposes of the human heart.

We were young and finding our way,
University chums hold special sway,

Each to each, the life of the mind
As important as girls. A fancied design

Of a future set in motion. You were
My best man. Forget what would

Come of it all. The kids, divorce.
You were essential. I'm not quite sure

What to make of a world without your essence.
Living leaves traces, points of reference

Not everyone understands. Memory requires
Verification. Extinguished fires,

A special kind of absence. A smudge,
A deeper darkness. I try to dial your number.

VI. John Devlin

Back when you and Peter still talked,
He appeared amused and then sulked;
My memory of how we had all met
Was backwards. Little matter now.
Love bore names and grew even
As things fell apart. We were not yet
Fully formed and learning how not to dream.

The scene was Park Avenue. History
Played itself out through war and peace,
The shadows of Zelda and Scott slowly
Erased by the fury of our time. Such
Immediacy robs youth of the romance
Of history. Still, surrender was never
In the plan. How easy it would have been!

A cigarette, a coffee, a pocket comb,
A cold beer. The list is endless. The plumb
Line. Your carpenter's tools. Oh, friend—
I see you with your camera, your rod
And reel, holding your daughter's hand.
How to gather you up in a song? I want
To ask, "Do you remember?" "Do you
Remember how we stood on Assateague's

Shore, waiting with our distant company,
Wondering how the ocean knew
To ravel and then untie our distant lure?

Lost Child

i. m. Darcy Kane

Sometimes in autumn, on street corners.
Sometimes at a broken place, the purposeless doors.
Sometimes the dust in a poor man's purse,
      And how he pays with dust,
      Which is memory.
Sometimes a child will pass this way,
Too soon, leaving only a fine trace,
Just touching air before settling out.
      So dust is a pity too—
And, still, Darcy, your name shines through.

Beautiful Envelopes of Morning

Will these beautiful envelopes
Conceal my faithlessness toward my fellows
And their disasters?

This morning afloat on the destiny of my sheets
Awaiting the new day, a wind
Whistles through golden passageways.
Moments willow away beneath their masks.
The detonations end at breakfast
When I discard my black eggs
And dredge up strength for sight.
Outside, the trees are as heavy
As Christ's tiaras.

It would be burdensome but for today's sun,
Its head emptied of promises.

To think that I am all here—
And after so many sad farewells!